PRAYERS & AFFIRMATIONS FOR YOUTHS

ANDRENE CUNNINGHAM

Prayers and Affirmation

All Scripture quotations, unless otherwise marked, are taken from The Holy Bible, New Living Translation, copyright ©1996, 2004, 2015 by Tyndale House Foundation. Used by permission of Tyndale House Publishers, a Division of Tyndale House Ministries, Carol Stream, Illinois 60188. All rights reserved.

Copyright © 2020 by Andrene Cunningham

The Cunningham Publishing Group, LLC

Book Cover: fiverr.com/nabinkarna

Barracks Editorial & Design House, LLC - iambevtheeditor@gmail.com

Graphic Image: www.robsteaching.com

All Rights Reserved. This book or any portion thereof may not be reproduced or used in any form or any manner whatsoever without the express written permission of the author except for the use of brief quotations in a book review. Please direct all inquiries to: acunningham1317@gmail.com.

ISBN-978-1-7347502-0-1

Printed in the United States of America

* * * * * * * * * * * *

Prayers and Affirmation

Introduction

*A*ffection. *P*rofession. *T*hanksgiving. *S*olicitation – **A.P.T.S**

I AM SO EXCITED TO SHARE THIS BOOK WITH YOU.

Do you know how to **PRAY**?

What is Prayer anyway?

Let me introduce you to the world of prayer. Some of you may have already been exposed to prayer, and others, not so much. Don't feel intimidated if this is your first time praying; I promise, it will be surprisingly very easy to do once you keep practicing.

Psalm 100:4.

"Enter his (God's) gates with thanksgiving; go into his courts with praise. Give thanks to him and bless his name." — **(paraphrased).**

Prayers and Affirmation

Table of Contents

INTRODUCTION..iii

A.P.T.S..1

AFFIRMATION...5

GIVING GOD THANKS.......................................7

A GOOD DAY..9

I AM VALUABLE..11

TEACH ME MY PURPOSE..................................13

PRAYING FOR MY PARENT/S..........................15

HAVING FRIENDS..17

BEING AN EXAMPLE..19

ASKING FOR WISDOM.....................................21

I AM VICTORIOUS...23

BLESS MY SCHOOL..25

FORGIVING OTHERS..27

Prayers and Affirmation

PRAYER OF SALVATION	29
NOTES	31
HOW TO WRITE YOUR REFLECTION	33
REFLECTIONS	34
GLOSSARY	48
REFERENCES	49

Prayers and Affirmation

A – AFFECTION (display of love, vocal expression of love).

P – PROFESSION (declaration of sin, pride, misbehavior etc.)

T – THANKSGIVING (gratitude, appreciation to God).

S – SOLICITATION (requests, appeals, petitions for yourself, family, friends).

<u>AFFECTION</u> – Speak words of Love to God. Tell Him how much you love Him.

Prayer:

Heavenly Father, You are Great, You are Awesome, You are Grand, You are Breathtaking, You are Marvelous, You are Gracious, You are Tremendous, You are Splendid, All Knowing, All Powerful, Everlasting. There is no one like You. You are Strong and Mighty, Omnipotent (having unlimited Power, able to do anything), Omniscient (knowing everything), Omnipresent (Ever-present), I give you Praise!

In Jesus Name! Amen!

<u>PROFESSION</u> – Admitting to God that you have missed the mark and made some mistakes.

Prayer:

Heavenly Father, I come before You to confess my sins; anything that I have said, done or thought about that is not of you. Your Word says, *"If I confess my sins, You are Faithful and Just to forgive me of my sins and cleanse me from all wickedness."* **(1 John 1:9).**

Prayers and Affirmation

Now, name the things that you did that you know did not please God. For example, lying, stealing, cursing, sexual sin, not respecting your parents and/or teachers. Include, anything else you can think of.

I receive your forgiveness today. I thank You Lord for Your forgiveness.

In Jesus Name. Amen!

THANKSGIVING — Giving God thanks for life, people, and possessions you have been blessed with.

Prayer:

Heavenly Father, I thank You for life, my family, my friends, my school, my church, my neighbors, and all the people that work to keep us safe. I thank You for food to eat and clothes to wear. I thank You for the opportunity to be a witness to others of Your Goodness, Mercy and Grace. I thank You that when faced with difficult decisions, Lord, You give me the correct thing to say and the do. I bless You because you knew who I was before I was formed in my mother's womb. I thank you for making me unique *(I am like no one else; I am special to You)*, I give YOU Glory; I give YOU Honor. There is no one like YOU in all the World. I Love YOU Lord, and I thank YOU for loving me. Lord, you have always been good to me, and for that I say Thank You.

SOLICITATION — Ask God for your desires, dreams, hopes. Pray!

Prayer:

Heavenly Father, I thank You for the opportunity to come before You and make my requests known to You. I pray that You would bless me

Prayers and Affirmation

with wisdom, knowledge and quick understanding. That the eyes of my understanding be enlightened, so that I can understand what You have in store for my life. Help me to always demonstrate the right attitude, and behavior, and speak the correct words, representing You in all the things I do. Help me to assist my family with being and staying close to You. Let me be an excellent athlete, exemplary student, friend and sibling. Give me the wisdom to be a young entrepreneur who will be Blessed to be a Blessing to the Kingdom of God. Help me to serve You God, and not money because if I put You first in ALL things, You will in return give me my heart's desire *(Psalm 37:4)*–(paraphrased).

Now that we have covered the foundation of prayer, let's get into the learning how to pray. Some people pray first thing in the morning after they wake up, others find it more convenient to pray at nights before bed; and still, others say prayers while in the car on their way to school or work. Whatever time you choose, just ensure it's a quiet space for you and God only.

Prayers and Affirmation

AFFIRMATIONS:

Speaking God's truth about Yourself

It is important to speak well of or affirm oneself in Christ.

- I am fearfully and wonderfully made
- I am smart
- I am strong
- I can do all things in Christ who strengthens me
- I am healthy
- I am wealthy, I create generational wealth
- I am wise
- I am consistent
- I am trustworthy
- I am persistent
- I complete my daily assignment by God
- I will accomplish all my dreams and aspirations
- I am bold in Christ
- I am passionate about my future
- I deserve to be in the room
- I have favor with God and man
- I excel in school
- I study and retain what I study
- I am creative

Prayers and Affirmation

- I am innovative
- I am a leader and not a follower
- I lend to many and borrow from no one
- I study the Word of God to show myself approved
- I am joyful
- I am peaceful
- I am gentle
- I am kind to all
- I am meek and humble
- I am a Philanthropist
- I am a Missionary of the Gospel of Jesus Christ
- I am a prayer

Prayers and Affirmation

GIVING GOD THANKS

Father,

I thank You for today. I thank You that You are GOD all by Yourself. I thank You God that You sent Jesus Christ to die on the cross for my sins. This is the day that You have made, I shall rejoice and be glad in it. I give You thanks, that my body, my organs and my mind, functions as they should. I thank You God, that today will be a prosperous and a productive day. I give my life to You, to guide and direct it as You like today. I thank You for my school/work. I thank You for my angels that have gone before me and have made my path safe. Give me the strength Oh God to do Your will.

It's in Jesus Name I pray. AMEN!

Psalm 118:24

Luke 4:10

Romans 5:8

Philippians 4:13

Prayers and Affirmation

A GOOD DAY

Father,

I thank You that today will be a good day. I thank You God, that any trap of the enemy that has been set for me to fail, miss the mark or not accomplish my goals or dreams for today, will not prosper because GOD You are my protection. I will exercise patience, show kindness, and work hard at everything I do. I am a child of God and I am victorious. Whatever I learn today, anything I experience today, will all work for my good in life. I choose to be positive and optimistic; I will not allow negative or mean things to come out of my mouth or fester in my thoughts; You GOD will defend me. Today, I have more than enough wisdom, knowledge, and quick understanding to be productive and successful in all that I do.

In the matchless Name of Jesus. AMEN!

Psalm 31:4

Galatians 6:9

Daniel 1:17

Prayers and Affirmation

I AM VAULABLE

Father,

When I think about Your goodness, and all You have done for me, my soul cries HALLELUJAH! YOU, Oh LORD knew me from before I was formed in my mother's womb. You fashioned me after Your Own Image and likeness; YOU formed my inner parts. YOU had a plan for my life even before then. A plan to prosper me and not harm me, a plan to give me hope and a future. I praise YOU because I am fearfully and wonderfully made. YOU know my thoughts even before I formed them in my mind. YOU supply the birds of the air with their every need. I know I am more valuable to You than the birds; therefore, I give You praise because I am valuable to YOU. God, because you are my Shepherd, I am not in need of anything.

In Jesus Name. Amen!

Genesis 1:27

Psalm 139:13

Matthew 6:25

Prayers and Affirmation

TEACH ME MY PURPOSE

Father,

Teach me how to number my days; for I am sure that all things work together for good for those who love God and are called according to HIS purpose. God I am grateful that You have called me according to YOUR will and purpose. Teach me Your way, LORD, that I may rely on Your faithfulness. Give me an undivided heart, that I may fear YOU. Hear my cry, Oh Lord, and show me Your perfect will for my life. Give me an ear to hear what you are saying to my spirit man so that this way LORD, I will not miss Your commands for my life.

In Jesus Name. Amen!

I Samuel 3:10

Psalm 86:11

Romans 8:28

Revelation 3:22

Prayers and Affirmation

PRAYING FOR MY PARENT/PARENTS

Father,

Your word says that I should "Honor my father and mother so that my days may be long on the Earth. Today, I pray for my parent/parents. I pray Almighty God that You would keep them from danger, and give them the wisdom they need to raise Godly children. Provide for them by giving them promotions on their job, successful businesses, good business deals, being a strong Influence in the community and most of all, a great example in our home.

I pray for my dad, that he will be a mighty man of valor, loving, caring and kind to us. I pray that he will teach us how to pray and touch the throne room of God. I pray You will give him wisdom on how to lead at home and at work. I pray Lord, that You will keep him in all Your ways. Heal him from all past hurts and pain and give him a new lease on life. Let him be happy in You. In Jesus Name!

I pray for my Mom, that she will be able to provide be the strength and support our family needs. I thank You Lord that she has eyes to see, and ears to hear when the enemy tries to sneak into our family. I pray that she will do well on her job, in her business and at home.

In Jesus Name! Amen!

I pray that my parents will have a relationship that is pleasing to You, God. Sanctify and keep them holy for Your purpose and Glory. Speak

Prayers and Affirmation

individually to their hearts. Teach them how to love each of their children differently (according to that child's need). Lord, let them be an example to me and my siblings, exemplifying the Fruits of the Spirit (Love, Joy, Peace, Patience, Kindness, Goodness, Faithfulness, Gentleness and Self-Control.)

In Jesus Name. Amen!

Exodus 20:12

Judges 6:12

Proverbs 22:6

Galatians 5:22-23

Prayers and Affirmation

HAVING FRIENDS

Father,

I thank You for the privilege of having friends. Help me Oh Lord to apply wisdom when choosing my friends. I pray that the person that becomes my friend will love me like I love them, look out for me, as I look out for them, protect me, as I protect them. Even though Lord we may not always agree, I pray for the spirit of unity that will hold our friendship together during the hard times.

Lord, I pray that my friend will be able to come to me for support and Godly counsel, as I will be able to go to them the same. Teach me to love others, the way You first loved me.

Lord, open my eyes to see when others will try to cause strife between us. Let me never retaliate in the flesh because Your word says, "vengeance is Mine, I shall repay." So, Lord, let me be confident that You love me enough, that when I come to You with challenges in my friendships, You hear me and respond.

I pray that there will be no strife, bad mouthing, deception, animosity or rebellion in my friendships. I pray that we will always encourage each other and build up one another in Christ.

In Jesus Name. Amen!

Psalm 133:1
Proverbs 12:26
Proverbs 27:9
Galatians 6:2

Prayers and Affirmation

BEING AN EXAMPLE

Father,

I thank You for wisdom, knowledge and quick understanding to know what to do at the correct time. YOU said YOU would never leave me or forsake me. I pray that when I find myself in situations and circumstances that are not pleasing to YOU Oh God, YOU will help me find a way to remove myself from it.

I pray that I will not become a stumbling block for any person, saved or unsaved. Let me be a witness for YOU, for the Grace and Mercy YOU have shown me. Teach me to Love, be Patient, Kind, and Forgiving to others, just as YOU are to me. I thank YOU for Your Love.

In Jesus Name. AMEN!

Daniel 1:17

Ephesians 4:32

Philippians 4:13

Prayers and Affirmation

ASKING FOR WISDOM

Father,

I thank YOU that the fear of the Lord is the beginning of knowledge, but fools hate wisdom and instruction. I am not wise in my own eyes because I reverence You, Oh, Lord and I stay away from evil. If I do not forsake wisdom then she will protect me. I love wisdom and she watches over me. The FEAR of the Lord is the beginning of wisdom and though it cost me all I have; I will get understanding. I will please YOU GOD; and in return You will give me wisdom, knowledge and happiness. And to the sinner, You, God have given the task of gathering and storing up wealth to give it over to me because my life is pleasing to You, Oh, Lord. I thank You GOD for Your wisdom.

In Jesus Name! Amen!

Ecclesiastics 2:26

Proverbs 1:7

Proverbs 3:7

Proverbs 4:6-7

Prayers and Affirmation

I AM VICTORIOUS

Father,

I thank You that I am Your child; and because I am Your child, I can defeat the evil of this world and can discern my friends from my enemies by my Faith in You. For I know Lord that You go with me daily and fight for me against mine enemies to give me Victory. I understand that temptation will come; but You Lord are Faithful. You will not allow temptation to overtake me; for I know when temptation comes, You have already made a way of escape and given me the strength to endure. I will put on the whole armor of God (helmet, breastplate, shield, belt and shoes) daily, so that I can stand my ground against evil. And after doing all I can to stand, I will stand In You.

In Jesus Name. Amen!

Deuteronomy 20:4

Ephesians 6:13

I Corinthians 10:13

I John 5:4

Prayers and Affirmation

BLESS MY SCHOOL

Father,

I come to You today, asking You to bless my school. I know Your Word says, the Lord of Hosts is with me, the God of Jacob is my stronghold and because of that I feel secure. I pray for peace in my school. I pray that the teachers, staff, students and parents will be kind towards each other. I pray that we learn in every class the lessons that are being taught. I pray for patience and grace for the teachers, staff, volunteers, principal. Protect my school from the enemy, and people who will try to cause harm to us. I plead the Blood of Jesus over my school. Evil shall not come near us. Lord, help everyone to first submit to You, Your ways, Your will, and assist us to submit to the authority of the school.

In Jesus Name. Amen!

Psalm 46:11

Psalm 91:7

Romans 13:1

Prayers and Affirmation

FORGIVING OTHERS

Father,

You said in Your Word, I am to love my enemies, bless them that curse me and do good to them that hate me. Pray for them that despitefully use me and persecute me. Lord, these things are hard for me right now. But if You command me to do these things, it means You have already given me the power to forgive all the people that have hurt me. I pray that You, Oh God, soften my heart to be able to love those who have hurt me, unfriended me, stolen from me, embarrassed me. Lord, as I forgive them, I pray You continue to forgive me of my sins. Give me the right words to speak to them in love. Help me to release them from my heart, so that I do not give an open door to the enemy to creep in and cause my heart to be hardened.

In Jesus Name I pray. Amen!

Matthew 5:44

Matthew 6:12

Ephesians 4:32

Prayers and Affirmation

Prayer of Salvation

Father,

According to **Romans 10:9-13** *(Speak this aloud):*

"If I confess with my mouth that Jesus is Lord and believe in my heart that God raised Him from the dead, I will be saved. For it is by believing in my heart that I am made right with God, and it is by confessing with my mouth that I am saved. You, Lord, gives generously to all who call on You. If I trust in You God, I will never be disgraced." I repent, for I am a sinner. I ask You to forgive me of my sins. Today, I receive You as my Savior and Lord. I turn my back on the things of this world, and I look now whole-heartedly unto You. I willingly give You my life, soul, mind and heart. I invite the Holy Spirit to come and dwell in me. Create in me a clean heart Oh, God and renew a right spirit within me. Thank You for receiving me as Your Own.

In Jesus Christ Name I pray. Amen!

WELCOME TO THE BODY OF CHRIST.
You are now a born-again follower of

Jesus Christ

Prayers and Affirmation

NOTES

As you practice praying, you will start to feel the need to spend more time with God. **GREAT!!**

Here is a list of tools you should bring to your Prayer Time:

1. Bible (to look up the scriptures).

2. Notebook (to write what you hear the Holy Spirit speak to you).

3. Pen or Pencil (your personal choice).

4. Worship music (to help set the atmosphere to enter into the Presence of God).

Prayers and Affirmation

How to write your Reflection(s)

The following pages are left blank for you to write your reflections after making your daily confessions. Think about it as reflecting on how your day went after praying and reading the Word of God.

Prayers and Affirmation

REFLECTIONS

Day: _____
Month/Day/Year: _____
Time: _____
Thoughts/Revelation/Illumination:

Prayers and Affirmation

Day: _____
Month/Day/Year: _____
Time: _____
Thoughts/Revelation/Illumination:

_____
_____
_____
_____
_____
_____
_____
_____
_____
_____
_____
_____
_____
_____
_____
_____
_____

Prayers and Affirmation

Day: _____
Month/Day/Year: _____
Time: _____
Thoughts/Revelation/Illumination:

Prayers and Affirmation

Day: _____
Month/Day/Year: _____
Time: _____
Thoughts/Revelation/Illumination:

Prayers and Affirmation

Day: _____
Month/Day/Year: _____
Time: _____
Thoughts/Revelation/Illumination:

Prayers and Affirmation

Day: _____
Month/Day/Year: _____
Time: _____
Thoughts/Revelation/Illumination:

Prayers and Affirmation

Day: _____
Month/Day/Year: _____
Time: _____
Thoughts/Revelation/Illumination:

Prayers and Affirmation

Day: _____
Month/Day/Year: _____
Time: _____
Thoughts/Revelation/Illumination:

Prayers and Affirmation

Day: _____
Month/Day/Year: _____
Time: _____
Thoughts/Revelation/Illumination:

Prayers and Affirmation

Day: _____
Month/Day/Year: _____
Time: _____
Thoughts/Revelation/Illumination:

_____
_____
_____
_____
_____
_____
_____
_____
_____
_____
_____
_____
_____
_____
_____
_____
_____

Prayers and Affirmation

Day: _____
Month/Day/Year: _____
Time: _____
Thoughts/Revelation/Illumination:

Prayers and Affirmation

Day: _____
Month/Day/Year: _____
Time: _____
Thoughts/Revelation/Illumination:

_____
_____
_____
_____
_____
_____
_____
_____
_____
_____
_____
_____
_____
_____
_____
_____
_____
_____
_____

Prayers and Affirmation

Day: _____
Month/Day/Year: _____
Time: _____
Thoughts/Revelation/Illumination:

Prayers and Affirmation

Day: _____
Month/Day/Year: _____
Time: _____
Thoughts/Revelation/Illumination:

Prayers and Affirmation

GLOSSARY

- Blood of Jesus – is a weapon; it destroys the works of the enemy
- Grace – free and unmerited favor of God
- Hallelujah – God be Praised, the Highest Praise
- Lord of Host(s) – Army of Angels
- Mercy – compassion or forgiveness shown towards someone
- Missionary – one sent to promote Christianity in a foreign country
- Philanthropist – a person who seek(s) to promote others, especially by the generous donation of money to good causes
- Reflections – serious thought or consideration
- Salvation – deliverance from sin and its consequences; only found in Jesus Christ
- Stronghold – fortress; hold

Prayers and Affirmation

REFERENCES

1. New Living Translation Bible

2. Oxford English Dictionary **www.oed.com**

www.ingramcontent.com/pod-product-compliance
Lightning Source LLC
Chambersburg PA
CBHW061259040426
42444CB00010B/2432